T0148013

L.O.R.T.E.

(Levels of Response to Traumatic Events)

A Vital Aid in Serving Children of Incarcerated Parents

JOYCE DIXSON-HASKETT

iUniverse, Inc.

New York   Bloomington

iUniverse books may be ordered through booksellers or by contacting:

iUniverse
1663 Liberty Drive
Bloomington, IN 47403
www.iuniverse.com
1-800-Authors (1-800-288-4677)

Because of the dynamic nature of the Internet, any Web addresses or
links contained in this book may have changed since publication and may
no longer be valid. The views expressed in this work are solely those of
the author and do not necessarily reflect the views of the publisher, and
the publisher hereby disclaims any responsibility for them.

ISBN: 978-1-4502-1762-0 (sc)
ISBN: 978-1-4502-1763-7 (ebook)

Printed in the United States of America

iUniverse rev. date: 03/03/2010

Forward

One of the most rapidly growing populations in our country is that of children of prisoners. It is my ultimate desire to provide a model by which caregivers, foster parents, grandparents, case workers, judges, teachers and anyone else who works with this population, can provide a more effective and unified method of working with this group.

This is not a segmented problem; it's a national problem that requires national attention. We need the help of policy makers, public health administrators, teachers and community leaders in addition to the families who are already doing everything they know how to do.

We need productivity and efficiency in the way we design programs for this group. Hopefully the LORTE Model (Levels of Response to Traumatic Events) will become a vital aid in the undertaking of this great task.

Introduction

This is a handbook to aid individuals in understanding the LORTE Model and how it works. **L**evels of **R**esponse to **T**raumatic **E**vents, or heretofore referred to as LORTE was created for:

- Family members who have an incarcerated loved one

- Caregivers who are raising children of prisoners

- Professionals who work with this population; and

- For anyone who desires to understand children of incarcerated parents and the circumstances by which they live.

Hopefully this handbook will provide insight and information that will allow you to be effective and successful while engaging this unique population.

I
Preface

The incarceration of a loved one can devastate, change the make-up of or in some cases— destroy an entire family unit. I chose to write this booklet because there are too many people, who do not understand how to relate, work with, interact with; or live with kids who have lost parents to prison. Understanding the principles and circumstances that most often govern the behavior of this population, will allow us to play an effective role in adding richness to their lives; and we can teach them how to keep it.

I am a clinical social worker by profession. I am also a wife and mother. I am very proud of that. I have also been an incarcerated mother. I am not proud of that. But the experience is a large part of who I have become and the reason for creating this model and this handbook. Many of the products, programs or services we use today are a direct result of a life changing transition or event that altered someone's life. In fact the LORTE Model came into existence because of a shattering personal experience in my own life. In order for you to fully understand the origin of LORTE, why it is necessary and why it is so dear to my heart, I will have to share some of those experiences. They aren't happy ones. The cutting ones never are, but if they don't kill you, they really will make you stronger for tomorrow.

PART ONE

The Act

II

Declaration

I shot a man. I killed him dead. I was prepared to go to prison for what I had done. What I was not prepared for was what this would do to my children.

PART TWO

The Response

III

End or Beginning: Beginning or End?

"Joyce Dixson, I find you guilty of Murder in the first Degree, and sentence you to spend the rest of your natural life in prison."

That was what the judge said to me on that dreadful day in August of 1976.

As I stood there in the courtroom, I listened to the verdict and sentence and in bewildered disbelief I wondered: "How could my life have come to this?"

The next thing that I wondered was: "What is going to happen to my children?"

PART THREE

Precursor

IV

Hindsight

I had lots of dreams as a little girl. Going to prison was never one of them. However it happened, I killed a man. I should have gotten away from him long before it happened: But like so many women in situations like those, I was caught up; in way over my head and didn't know how to get out. So I stayed. I was 25 years old with two children six and eight years old. He wasn't their father. He wasn't even a father figure. He was a womanizer and he was very good at it.

I realized before long that I had gotten myself into a mess and didn't know how to get out. How familiar is that phrase to us? He was older and much more experienced than I was. His job was to know women. They were his prey; his livelihood. He knew how inexperienced, how vulnerable and how needy I was; and he knew how to handle me. He was also a bully. I was afraid of him and he knew it. Fear is a tool that many men use to control women with. Abusive men make it very clear to you that they are bigger, stronger and meaner. I was very afraid of him. My mother used to always say: "The last person you want to keep messing with is a scared person because they are the ones who are the most unpredictable." I understand that now because you cannot measure a person's level of fear; or what their reaction to it might be at any given time.

To get right to it; I shot him in late December1975 and he laid there and died before my eyes.

I didn't know anything about the law. I had never been in trouble; had never even been inside a court room before that time. I had a bench trial which means no jury. That was ridiculous. I was on trial for Murder in the First Degree; on trial for my life. To not have a jury trial was insane. However, it was what my attorney recommended. I trusted him. That is another story and was another huge mistake.

When the short trial was over I had been found guilty of Murder in the First Degree and sentenced to spend the rest of my natural life in prison. I had killed a man. I was prepared to go to prison. I was not prepared for a natural life sentence; and most importantly, I was not prepared for what this was going to do to my children.

V

My children were not in the courtroom that day. However, when I received my sentence, they were sentenced as well

Ostracized, labeled, devalued and outcast were just a few of the things that happened to my children when I was convicted of murder. How could this be? They had never done anything to anybody. They didn't shoot anybody. I did. Yet they were treated from the onset as if they committed the crime. I entered into a prison constructed from brick and mortar. They were imprisoned within a subculture constructed by narrow-mindedness, bigotry and prejudice. They now lived in a community that turned away from them instead of embracing them. Someone could have helped them simply by offering some encouragement; a few words of plain truth might have done the trick, like: "This is not your fault" perhaps. They were eight and six years old with no one to help them adjust to their new life without their mother; or aid them with the shock and trauma that enveloped them.

I, my mother, brother, and my two sons had always lived in the house with my grandmother and step grandfather. I was back and forth between my house and his. After the shooting, chaos was everywhere, especially in my grandmother's house. While the adults sat around talking and reacting to everything that was going on, no one was really talking to my sons. They were pretty much ignored while the family was adjusting to the situation. There was a lot of family chatter about the new situation; a lot of: "What are we going to do about this or that?" My children were pretty much ignored and excluded from those conversations. They were children and of course couldn't possibly understand what was truly going on. And since the family really didn't know how to help them; they simply filed them in the: "THEY WILL BE ALL RIGHT" category. This is a cover-all cliché people use when no one knows what to do or say.

They were far from being all right. No one took the time to try and explain to them what had happened and why. *They were too young to understand* is what I was told. They should have been given the chance to understand, especially since they were feeling the repercussions every day. In spite of what other people were saying about me, I was still their mother and they loved me. In the middle of the whispering by family and friends, they stood hurt, bewildered and confused. There was nothing I could do. I was sitting in the county jail waiting for my transfer and commitment papers to the Detroit House of Correction.

It is very interesting that upon my arrival at the prison, the old DeHoCo, (Detroit House of Correction), during the intake process, where you are asked to provide all your pertinent personal information-- and while I was asked questions like "what is your sexual preference and what is your religion: and do you have any tattoos or other identifying marks," (so they had some means to identify you in case you escaped), no one bothered to ask me about my children. I mean they didn't even ask if I had any children; or if I did have any whether or not they were being taken care of properly; or if they were receiving any kind of aid or support during my incarceration. There was absolutely no indication that the state had any concern for my children at all. Both I and my kids were on our own to find our way in a strange and cruel new world without any clues as to how to get through it. I mean we both could have used some sort of "How To" book: *"How to Survive Prison and Not Lose Your Life or Your Mind"* or a book entitled " *I'm a Kid and This is How to Survive in the Free World When My Mother is Locked Up."* Of course I am being sarcastic, well; perhaps I did mean it just a little bit. The point is we all needed help and we didn't get any. More specifically, they needed help and didn't get any. I am convinced, however, that a large part of the reason for that was that most people, lay and professional, weren't really equipped to provide them with what they needed. In order to help them one had to understand them; not so much the individual children but the circumstances under which children of incarcerated parents have to live. How the incarceration of a parent, especially the principle caregiver, affects the children as well as the community they dwell in. This includes family, the church, teachers, neighbors, social service agencies and the like. People must have some idea of how they feel, how they function and how they react to the reactions of others. This is a large order to fill, but it is not a difficult one when we have the right tools to work with. It really doesn't take a rocket scientist to figure out how to help or work effectively with these kids. It only takes some good information, time and care. If you have the time and the care, the good information will be supplied in the chapters to follow.

VI

Right and Left

My children were only two out of millions of children who have parents in prison. You're probably wondering how my children turned out; or more specifically what their lives progressed into as a result of my incarceration. My youngest son graduated from Eastern Michigan University. My oldest son has been serving a natural life sentence in prison for conspiracy to commit murder since he was barely out of his teens. So why did the lives of two brothers from the same household with the same hurts, pains and humiliations turn out so differently? Let's examine that and you be the judge.

VII

Flow of Information

A lot of what we do is a direct result of how we think. How and what we think are a direct result of how we access and process information. Children don't process information the same way adults do. Nevertheless they process. They think about "*stuff*" based on the other "*stuff*" that people tell them. They use what they have. Where did they get the information from? Will the information they get be true or will it be information that is false? And from whom will they get it? Who they get it from makes a difference. Will they get it from someone who loves and cares for them? Or will they get it from someone they know; but someone who doesn't particularly care for them; but who is someone they might believe? It could be the mean neighbor across the street for instance. That too makes a difference and it can do a lot of damage.

Once you think about those questions, you need to know the manner in which the information was given to them. Was it given to them in a loving and caring manner; or was it just thrown at them from someone being cruel and mean? It makes a serious difference. For the kids, it's the difference between taking the road to understanding and acceptance; or the road to anger, animosity and unforgiveness toward the incarcerated parent and possibly the rest of the world. If they get information that is helpful, it more than likely will aid in healthy processing. Healthy processing leads to healthier thoughts and/or conclusions that will make them feel better about themselves, their current situation and the people they love and care about. However, if they get bad information or worse, no information, then they are left to figure things out for themselves. So if they are already feeling badly about something or someone and they get bad information or no information at all, they process with what they have. The equation would look something like this: bad + bad = worse. My youngest son found someone during his middle school years who talked to him, mentored him and helped to explain things to him. Although already badly damaged socially and psychologically, he had someone who processed positively with him. The irony is that his mentor was a police officer: "Go figure." My oldest son didn't have that. Clinically one would view the scenario as positive intervention vs. no meaningful intervention at all. They both would have been good candidates for separate focus groups. However, as a mother, the diagnosis is clear: "My child was hurting and no one stepped up to help him. In the book *Turning Stones,* author Mark Parent wrote: "There is no system; there [are] only people. Children do not fall through the cracks; they fall through fingers." I agree. We all have both a moral and professional responsibility to help these children before they fall victim to the next generation of prisoners. They are worth paying attention to. They are definitely worth saving.

VIII
Resiliency

The number of children in our communities who have incarcerated parents is staggering. It is no secret that there are approximately 2 million or more of these children in the United States. The number is probably higher. However since there is no single agency designated for collecting data specific to this population, we cannot be accurate about the numbers. We do know that children who lose parents to incarceration, especially the principal caregiver (which is usually the mother) are forced to deal with a variety of emotions and life changing events simultaneously; things they are neither responsible for or have any control over. Fear, anxiety, anger, hurt, shame, guilt and displacement are just a few. Critical changes take place in the lives of these children. They begin to exhibit low self-esteem and withdraw themselves from friends and family. Their lives change drastically and very quickly. In most cases the changes are very adverse.

Herein lays the biggest problem: the changes occur more rapidly than the children's ability to adjust or adapt. They have a very difficult time. They are walking around with someone else's baggage, shouting: "This is not my stuff." They are hurting and feeling lost and confused. It is unfortunate that they have to carry this baggage, but the fact still remains that they have a parent in prison and the negative stigma which accompanies incarceration sadly blemishes the children and they live with

the negative effects daily. So in lieu of this our job is to aid
our children in being the best that they can be in spite of these
facts. We cannot undo what they have witnessed, suffered or
lived through. But we can teach them how to effectively cope
with the changes in their lives and equip them with a powerful
tool that will remain true to them for the rest of their lives—
resiliency. LORTE is a tool for resiliency. In order to give our
children what they need to "bounce back," the tools must be
available to professionals, lay people and family members; and
it must be incorporated into the programs designed to help
them.

PART FOUR

The Model

IX

The L.O.R.T.E. MODEL

I am a social worker by profession. In my experience, I have been employed by agencies who worked with kids with all kinds of problems. In those kinds of environments treatment plans had to be designed specifically for each individual youth in the program. These plans are specific and individual in theory, but not in real practice. The reality is that most of the goals and objectives had been prewritten. They were all in a "goal and objective" pool- so- to- speak. As the social worker assigned to the case, my job was to search the pool of prewritten goals and objectives and choose those I thought would be applicable for the kids on my case-load. The object, in essence, was to use a combination of goals and objectives (whatever we thought would work) in order to change, modify or induce the desired behavior; the "Multisystemic" plan of treatment. However, the behavior, of kids with incarcerated parents, wasn't the crux of the problem; it was just the outcome. In order to really help you had to look farther than the exhibited behavior. Unfortunately with too many agencies there is not a lot of time for that. There are too many kids per caseload and not enough workers. Having an incarcerated parent wasn't really seen as a unique situation that warranted any special attention. No one identified parental incarceration as a major trauma causing agent.

This is a unique population and the stigma of parental

incarceration covers the children with a negative cloud that seems to follow them through life. These effects have long arms and can reach far into the next generation. It is not our job to try and fix the children. Our job is to help them to be the best they can be in spite of the situation.

What is L.O.R.T.E?

L.O.R.T.E. is the acronym for Levels of Response to Traumatic Events. It is:

- A prevention tool to be incorporated into the design of programs for children of incarcerated parents

- A tool to aid in describing what their journey is like and the stops they will make along the way

- A tool that allows one to anticipate reactions and behaviors to emotional events

- A tool that allows the youth and the caregiver and/or professional to identify where the youth is in the cycle

What Does L.O.R.T.E. Do?

L.O.R.T.E.

- Defines, tracks and explains adverse behavior

- Describes the events, mechanisms and behaviors exhibited by youth who have incarcerated parents

- Simplifies the task of creating effective treatment goals

X

The Cycle

I have worked with many children who have incarcerated parents. I have talked extensively with them; and listened very closely to what they have said. I have talked with other family members and caregivers about the children. I have also spoken on several occasions to teachers and other professionals who work closely with this population. As a result it is my belief that children of incarcerated parents pass through four levels or stages of events, emotions and reactions during their parent's incarceration and absence. Therefore we work with the L.O.R.T.E. Model in four stages:

- Stage 1=Event (the actual arrest)
- Stage 2=Saturation
- Stage 3 =Blaming
- Stage 4=Outcome

The programs we design are based on a guide that will navigate you through each episode of change, and enable you to intelligently anticipate what will happen next. Understanding the stages and each of the events in the stages will provide a better insight into the youth's place in the cycle.

Stage 1-The Arrest

Physical Separation
Abandonment
Detachment
Invalid Belief System
Judicial System
Labeling

State 2-Saturation

Fear
Grief/Loss
Loneliness
Hurt/Pain
Hopelessness
Loss of Identity
Sense of Abandonment
Shame/Humiliation
Guilt/Responsibility

Stage 3-Blaming

Bottled Anger
Blame
Depression
Feels Victimized

Stage 4-Outcome

Incorrigibility
No Respect for Authority
Acting Out
Becomes Victimizer
Gang Involvement

PART FIVE

Stages

XI

Stage 1-The Event

- Shattered Belief System
- Physical Separation
- Judicial System
- Detachment/Abandonment
- Labeling

When we talk about Stage 1 or the "Event," we are talking about the actual arrest and its effects on children especially if they were present during the arrest. It is the place where concrete changes occur. From this point on, life as the children know it changes adversely and very quickly. Here the children are introduced to and experience such episodes as a shattered belief system, physical separation, the judicial system, abandonment, detachment and labeling.

Shattered Belief System

It wasn't until I began working with this group that I realized how fragile a belief system can be particularly where children are concerned. Although they are tough and probably more resilient than most adults, they are emotionally vulnerable. They are who we have taught them to be until they discover independent thinking. Let's use children ranging in age from 5-8 years old for the purpose of this illustration. By the time they reach the ages mentioned, they have been taught that they can and should trust different groups of people. We teach them that if they are sick; they can trust the doctor. When we need legal assistance; we can trust our lawyer. And if you ever need help, you can trust the police. We teach them that the police are their friends; that if they get lost a policeman will help them: That if someone needs help dial 911. They believe what we tell them. They even practice dialing 911 on the phone. They believe they can trust authority. Then one day the police come to the house. They kick the door down. They are screaming and yelling: "Everybody down on the floor face down." They are waving guns at everyone even the 8, 9 and 10 year olds. The children watch as the police handcuff their mother or father, then drag them out of the house into the street where all the neighbors are watching and then into the police car. They know they have done nothing wrong. Crying, afraid, confused and bewildered they watch as all they have been taught about the police, trust and authority vanish like a vapor. The little box that contained all their beliefs has been crushed into the dust. The worst part is, it's just beginning.

Physical Separation

The parent or parents have been arrested. A very important person in their lives has been taken from them. If it is the mother more than likely the children have lost their principle caregiver. It is difficult to say what other family members they may be separated from at this time. That depends on the ability and availability of other family members or extended family members to care of the rest of the children. So whose responsibility is it to make sure the remaining children are seen after once the parent is so abruptly removed from the home? What happens to those children?

I spoke to a policeman about that very same thing. He said

to me: "Joyce I would love to be able to say that we stay and make sure that all the kids are taken care of or until protective services arrives. But I can't say that to you." He said: "When we go into a home to arrest someone we know that we are walking into hostile territory. We have been trained to go in, do what we need to do and get out as quickly as possible without getting hurt or hurting anybody." "So what happens to them?" I asked. He said: "Many times they stay at the house until someone comes to pick them up. It's usually the grandmother. Or a neighbor or someone will stay with them or take the children to their house until some other family member comes and picks them up." So what do you (as the reader) think happens to these kids? Well your guess is about as good as any. My guess is that they go where they can.

Judicial System

Many children with incarcerated parents end up as part the judicial system either as wards of the court or in matters of guardianship. Too often the court doesn't even know the kids are out there until someone shows up with them because they need financial assistance to continue to care for them; or they cannot get them into school without showing proper guardianship. The courts see this all the time. One fact still amazes me however. When kids come through the courts for these kinds of reasons; I mean when they have just been pawns in someone else's mess, the reaction is always one of sympathy and sadness for the child. For example, one might say: "This child is only 6 years old. What a shame." But when the same kid, (after he's been bounced from home to home and suffered abuse after abuse) comes back through the same court at age 13 with a felony; the same court wants to charge him as an adult. No mercy or sympathy then. Now that is the real shame.

Detachment and Abandonment

Detachment should be expected after a child has been in and out of the courts, foster homes and schools, etc. He or she has already been separated from all they know and love. It's no wonder that they begin to show signs of disinterest in what happens to them, to you and the rest of the world. *"Why should I get attached to you when I know I'm going to be sent somewhere else very soon? Why should I let myself care about you when I know that you don't really care anything about me? You are just in this for the monthly check. I have been abandoned by the people who said they would never leave me: So why should I trust you?"* These are the kinds of thoughts that so easily attach themselves to the children. When one system replaces another, so does another set of thoughts, beliefs and values. So you may want to consider this when the children you are caring for or working with begin to "close down" on you or overtly place distance between you and them. It's not personal; or maybe it is. Whichever, they are protecting themselves from what they believe will only be another hurt or disappointment. They believe they are protecting themselves from you. The ability to detach becomes easier and easier.

Labeling

It's amazing how quickly people can rename you. In some instances it's called a "nick-name." At other times it's what I call "Labeling." Billy has been "Billy" to everyone in the neighborhood for as long as he has been in the neighborhood. One day his mom goes to jail and he's no longer identified as Billy, rather, he's identified as "the kid whose mom just went to jail or prison." Or he's identified with the crime that the parent committed. On occasion my children were identified as "the kids of the woman who killed so-in-so." It was very mean and very damaging.

Labels are negative attachments that only serve to help our children learn how to detach from family and friends quickly. There is a labeling theory (also known as social reaction theory) developed by Howard Becker. The theory says that deviance is not a quality of the act because it is the result of personality factors associated with committing deviance or the act. It focuses on the linguistic tendency of majorities to negatively label minorities or those seen as deviant from the norms. So even though the children haven't done anything wrong, they are labeled and classified as deviant. The theory is concerned with how the self-identity and behavior of individuals may be determined or influenced by the terms used to describe or classify them, and is associated with the concept of a self-fulfilling prophecy and stereotyping (Becker, Howard. Outsiders1963). New York, NY: Free Press.)

In this case, it is not the deviance of the children, but their parents. However, society too often associates or attaches one family member's mistake to everyone else in the family. They either hold them equally responsible or expect the patterns to be duplicated by the offspring. You know what they say: "The apple doesn't fall far from the tree." The travesty begins to unfold when the children start to believe the lie; begin to live up to the negative names they have been given; or begin to buy into the concept of the self-fulfilling prophecy that they too will become deviant. This one thing I know to be true. You are who you believe that you are.

XII

Stage 2-Saturation-Broken Heart Stage

Stage 1, or the Event is the place where children can somewhat see, identify and explain most of what has happened to them thus far. Though they may not be able to grasp such terms as "shattered belief system" or "labeling," they can tell you: "I don't believe the police are my friends; and "people are calling me names." They may not have the terminology but they get the gist of it. However level 2 is all about feelings and emotions; probably the most dangerous level of them all. Here they are bombarded with a plethora of feelings and emotions that they cannot identify, put a name with, connect to, or combat.

- Fear
- Grief/Loss (Ambiguous)
- Loneliness
- Hurt/pain
- Hopelessness
- Loss of Identity
- Sense of Abandonment
- Shame & Humiliation
- Guilt and Responsibility

Fear

The fear of **what happens next** can be overwhelming. This kind of fear is new to them; it's frightening and it's relevant. What's going to happen to my mother in prison? Is she going to be all right or are people going to hurt her? Is she now, officially, a "bad" person? What's going to happen to me and to my brothers and sisters? Where are we going to go? Who will we live with? How will people treat us? Will we all be together or will we be separated? What will all our friends think? Will we still have friends? They may not be able to articulate what they feel but they sense at the onset that danger and evil are imminent. And they are right.

These are all valid questions that children shouldn't have to try and figure out by themselves. If we say things to them like: "It's gonna be all right" or "don't worry because it will all work out," than we need to back those words up with a reason for them to believe what we say is true. Or else they will only be empty words to them. They will believe that we gave them the; *it will be okay* line only because we had nothing else to say. That doesn't help them feel more secure about their situation. We must find ways to diminish their fears not add to them.

Grief/Loss (Ambiguity)

Many people categorize the grief of children who've lost parents to incarceration as the same as children whose parents are divorced. Yes both groups grieve and have suffered loss. But it is quite different. The stigma of "disgrace" which is attached to someone who goes to prison is what separates the two.

We know that divorce is as common in this country as incarceration is. However divorce is socially acceptable. Imprisonment is not. But just as divorce is not the fault of the child; neither is the incarceration of a parent. Nevertheless, people treat the children of the incarcerated as if they committed the crime; as if it is somehow a gene that is passed down from generation to generation and that crime, punishment and imprisonment are inevitable; or worse; that it is a contagious disease that infects anyone that gets too close to these children.

The loss for these children can be very ambiguous. Particularly in terms of how some children view the loss. For example: I was serving a natural life sentence in prison. Some people had the gall to tell my children that it might be easier for them if they just pretended that I was dead; that they should just forget about me because I was never coming home; that I would never ever live or be with them again. How can people be so *stupid*? So my children were very unclear in how they should think of me. Herein lays the ambiguity. When someone dies there is finality to that. You know they are not coming back, well at least in this life. My children knew that I was not dead. I was absent in the body meaning I wasn't physically with them, but ever present in their minds because they knew I was alive and well. I just wasn't home. They would not have been so confused in that situation if only some thinking individual would have explained that to them. Or it would have been nice if someone had said something like: "As long as there is life there is hope." Hope is the one thing that you don't want kids to lose. Mom and dad may be in prison, but their lives still have their own destiny and purpose. Purpose and possibility should always be emphasized and encouraged.

Hurt/Pain

We certainly don't have to spend much time on these two. All we have to do is imagine what it feels like to suffer what they suffered through. Imagine losing your mother to prison;

being torn apart from your brothers and sisters; being bounced
from foster home to foster home; used, sometimes beaten
and molested and told that you're nothing at all because of
something that your parent did. Does thinking about it hurt?
It sure does. Just thinking about it may cause you to feel pain.
It is because none of us want to think of children who are
hurting that badly. The only things kids this age should have
to be worrying about are things like what they are going to
wear to school the next day; or is their homework done: or
when are they going to get their new IPOD. They should not
have to be worried about if they are going to survive or not.
We can't go back and erase all of that for them: But we can
try and help them understand that all of our experiences good
and bad make up who we are and eventually will be. The way
we use our experiences is up to us. We must teach them that
these kinds of experiences serve to make us stronger and better
for tomorrow. That will help both them and us.

Hopelessness

It is easy to feel helpless and "hopeless" when you believe
you have no control over your own life. Too many people are
making choices for you which seem to only benefit them. This
is the way many of these children feel. There are thousands of
children in foster homes and other placement facilities who
believe that the choices being made for them are only made to
insure that the agency bed is filled and the checks or stipends
continue to come. Don't get me wrong. There are a lot of
good people out there doing right by these children and any
other children in their care. But those families and homes
are far and few in between. Hopelessness is when you have
nothing, absolutely nothing to look forward to. Hopelessness
is when you want to tell someone how you are feeling; you
want to tell them about your sadness; or when someone has
done something mean or hurtful to you. But you don't even

bother to tell anyone because you know no one will listen to you—because the feeling of unimportance has become too attached to you. No child anywhere should ever have to feel that way. A hopeless child will grow into a desensitized adult who won't feel one way or another about **hurting you!** We are witnessing firsthand the creation of an intolerant, insensitive and potentially unpromising generation of youth. The question is: "How much of the responsibility for this generation is ours?" It may not be our intention to add to the despondency that some of these children already emulate. But when we pretend that the children of prisoners are not our problem; or that it's not our concern because it's the parent's fault that they went to prison; then we are closing our eyes to a huge problem that is brewing, profusely, right smack-dab in the middle of our communities. Therefore it is in our best interest to get involved when opportunity permits. If we do nothing else, we can encourage our youth to continue to make positive steps toward a better future even if they don't see it yet.

Loss of Identity

Loss of identity becomes evident to these unsuspecting and unprepared victims. Children who once had the presence of their parent in the home are now are trying to find their place in a strange home or facility, often with a strange family or just plain strangers. Who am I and how do I fit in quickly come into play.

Attending a new school often comes with a new place to live. Old friends are gone and these kids are very skeptical about making new ones. They don't want anyone to know their true circumstances; because if the other kids knew they had a parent in prison, then the likelihood is they would be flagged and labeled at the onset; and more than likely not readily accepted by other students. That is true more times than not.

It's amazing that no matter how hard we try and hide things from people, there is always someone who knows something about us. Another sad truth is that these people love to tell other people your business particularly if it is gossip that is negative or perceived by the bearer as "juicy." Kids in school can be very cruel. That is why we must prepare the children of the incarcerated for such cruelties. Of course no one can prevent people from saying what they want. Still, if prepared correctly, mean talk and gossip about them and/or their parent won't send them all the way over the edge, because they will know how to handle it. There may be some reaction, but it won't be over exaggerated. Although the reaction will still be somewhat negative; somewhat is better than an all out release of anger. Keeping negative reactions to a minimum is actually a plus.

XIII

Stage 3-Blaming

- Blame
- Victimization
- Bottled Anger
- Depression

We have talked about Stage I, The Event where most of the concrete changes take place; the actual arrest; physical separation, judicial system, etc. We have talked about Stage II, Saturation or The Broken Heart Stage where the children really try and figure out what is happening to them and why. Now we move to Stage III where the activation of dormant aggression begins.

Victimization and Blame

It stands to reason that when these children have been lonely, grieving, uprooted and unstable that their emotions soon shift to something else. They understand that they are not responsible for what their parent did. They know that they are just victims of their parent's bad choices and decisions. And since they didn't commit any crime then they conclude that what has happened to them is someone else's fault. They blame the parent and everyone else they can think of who may have had anything to do with their current situation.

Blame becomes prevalent. What is dangerous here is the degree to which their blame has ascended. Of course they are going to blame some people and have a right to. Still have they placed their blame where it belongs: Or have they lost all perspective and have begun to blame everyone for everything; and no longer assume any responsibility for acts they committed that might have contributed negatively to their situation? Blame becomes a quest and a fuel for disaster. Without positive intervention blame can be responsible for an enormous amount of aggression toward other unsuspecting and undeserving victims. When we live with, work with or just interact with one of these kids; and we see that they are falling into a pattern of blaming everything on someone or something else, then we need to step in and at least bring the pattern to their attention. As long as a sense of responsibility remains so does the belief that they still have a certain amount of control over their own lives. We want to help them build on that rather than watch them get lost in the "Blame Game." This is a game that they cannot win.

Bottled Anger

Have you ever been so angry that you felt like the top of your head was going to blow off? So angry that you could literally feel that big vein in the middle of your forehead pulsating? Yes, that one. Many of these kids feel like that. However they don't know how to positively channel the anger; neither do they have a safe place for release. So they carry most of it inside. Angry is a nicer version of what they really call it. They won't tell you that they are angry. They will tell you that they are "***mad***." One young lady told me: "I'm not angry, I'm mad as hell." That's pretty angry. That kind of anger can only be held within for so long until it begins to shift to something else. When that anger is not controlled it has the potential of doing great damage to others as well as the youth. It tells the mind it's time to fight.

The body follows suit. If that anger is not managed, than that person is almost always in a state of aggression and defense. Explosions of anger are unpredictable and occur often. And when the anger explosions are not displayed or apparent then there is a great risk of "Anger Repression or Bottled Anger." Bottled anger causes depression and anxiety. Personally that is the one which is most dangerous. You can't see it or measure it. You know it's there, but you have no idea if, when or how it's going to blow. All you know is that it will manifest itself at some point. My mother used to always say: "What's in is coming out and what's down is coming up." We want to help them learn how to express anger appropriately. It's healthier for them and for us.

Depression

Many of the experts say that these children may be more irritable and easy to anger. As a result they may show a reduced tolerance of the normal behaviors of peers and family members and produce a readiness to respond with aggression. However in my experience they shift first to depression before outward aggression. The depression is subtle nevertheless overwhelming. The depression is often undetected or over looked because it has not been identified by either the child or the caregiver. Most don't recognize the symptoms of childhood depression; particularly with this group of children. The signs are missed or ignored because whatever is going on with these kids is contributed to the situation. It is assumed that what they are going through is a normal result of the parent's incarceration. Most caregivers equate "depression" as just being a little down because of the circumstances; not as "depression," in the medical or clinical sense; a treatable disorder." So the children are left on their own to get through it.

They, the children, know they feel badly but can't attribute it to any specific thing. You know that something is wrong, and when you ask: "***What's wrong?*" *They say: "Nothing; or I don't know.*"* The truth is they don't know because they are unable to put a name with what it is they are feeling. They don't understand terms such as depression or symptoms; or phrases like social withdrawal. They can't really articulate why they are so angry or why they sometimes have thoughts of suicide. So, it's all just there and continues to be there until it shifts to something else. We call it "Eruption."

XIV

Stage 4-Eruption:

The Manifestation of Negative Behavior

- Acting Out
- Incorrigibility
- Lack of Respect for Authority
- Gang Involvement
- Victimizer

We could not think of a better way to describe this phase than by using a volcano to illustrate what happens to unstable kids when the top blows off[1]

Acting Out In School

Studies have shown that children of offenders struggle in school with poor performance both academically and behaviorally. That should not be a surprise to anyone. It is difficult to concentrate on studies when the children are concentrating on issues more important to them like:

- Where am I going to live

---

1   An actual volcano is used in our model and in all workbooks when illustrating this stage.

- What is happening to my incarcerated mother or father

- What is going to happen to me, my brothers and my sisters?

The trauma of losing a parent to prison also interferes with the process of learning to control emotions; which lets us know that aggressive behaviors and attention/concentration difficulties lead to academic and disciplinary problems at school.

Incorrigibility and Lack of Respect for Authority

Many of the children I have worked with contribute their state of "incorrigibility" directly to the "lack of respect for authority." A lot of this goes back to when their parent was arrested, particularly if the child was present during this traumatic event. Of course we must consider the age of the child at the time as well. One thing we know for sure is that if what they witnessed was during early adolescence (11-14 years), the most overwhelming emotions were fear and anger. The older the child the greater the likelihood of more anger and more distrust. People tend to give less respect to people they don't trust. Distrust encourages detachment. When you feel detached from the system; or start to believe that it was designed to hurt you and not help you, then you don't have respect for it **or** for the people authorized to protect it. Many of these children hate the "system" or what they have come to believe that the system is. What you get from them are incorrigibility and lack of respect for authority as a result. That lack of respect isn't attached to one specific area or group of people. It applies to everyone. Although when you ask them what is important to them, they will tell you respect. I had a young man tell me that he would die for his respect although he didn't respect anyone. "Go figure." They have got it so twisted. But the good news is, we can help them sort out some the pieces and put them into the right places. I have learned that when they say things like: "I will die for mine" (respect), they are saying "I want to feel important and I want you to stop treating me like I'm worthless because of something my parents did." They are saying: "If you stop fighting me—I will stop fighting you."

Victimization and Gang Involvement

In Stage III we discussed how blaming and depression easily allow children of prisoners to feel victimized. In Stage IV we believe that without positive intervention they shift from the feeling of being victimized to becoming the victimizer.

Without meaningful intervention during Stages 1 through 4 victimization and gang involvement appear to be a natural flow of the process. Victimization as defined by many of our kids simply means:

1. *You don't care anything about me; so I don't care anything about you.*

2. *Sooner or later you are going to get me, so I'm going to get you first.*

Because of this kind of blanket thinking, kids align themselves with other kids like them. Some call these groups Gangs---A subculture so to speak which appears to offer them something that has been missing from their lives, **family.** This "new family" has been through circumstances similar to theirs. They have been disrespected, labeled as "losers", disregarded and thrown away by their communities. And they appear to meet another need that we seem to have missed or failed to provide. They offer Protection or a semblance of protection.

This may seem a little far-fetched by the reader; however you are what you believe you are. Too many of these children believe that we don't care about them and that they are out there on their own. So they act accordingly. But they are wrong. We do care about them. Therefore let us be more innovative and implement strategies and programs that they understand and relate too. That way they will know that they are not out there by themselves; and that they are not the only ones who know what they are truly going through.

PART SIX

Conclusion

XV

Behavior modification and mentorship programs alone aren't going to get it done. Without meaningful intervention and programs that address all the elements of the cycle, progression to the next level of intergenerational incarceration is almost inevitable. Overcoming these obstacles is not simple, but success is possible. Understanding this model will make it easier.

One Two Three Four

With time and experience you will learn to identify which of the four stages a child is in. Your understanding of the cycle will help the children you work with also understand the cycle. When they understand we are looking at more successes than failed attempts to connect and really help this population.

Our children really are our future: All of them. We need to do all we can to nurture and aid in their positive growth and development. When we write them off or refuse to accept any responsibility for their potential successes we throw away part of our future. Investing in their lives can only make our lives richer.

For more information please contact us at:

RWC Inc.
P.O. Box 33112
Bloomfield Hills MI 48303
248-225-2495 Phone
248-352-7900 Fax
rwc@comcast.net
www.lortemodel.org

Notes

Notes

Notes

Notes

Notes

Notes

Notes

Notes

Notes

Notes

Notes

Notes

Notes